My Pen Speaks
Poetic Mind Vibes

Patrice Watley-Williams

Strategic Book Group

Strategic Book Group
P.O. Box 333
Durham CT 06422
www.StrategicBookClub.com

ISBN: 978-1-60911-325-4

Book Design: Suzanne Kelly

Author's Web Site: http://www.poeticmindvibes.net

Table of Contents

iv PATRICE WATLEY-WILLIAMS

Reflections
and Special Thanks

Reflecting on life and thanking God first for allowing me to love him, to love and serve others by sharing and empowering people with my words of difficulties, confusion, love of life and continued perseverance of my journey to be a better person if only to leave a small, marked legacy behind. This is my contribution to paying it forward.

I must thank my family for their continued support, My husband Joseph Williams; my children Bobby and Akieria Hall and Zaire Williams; my mom Maxine Watley-Rowe; and my extended family. Hopefully they are proud as I turn my caterpillars into butterflies. Additionally, I want to thank Connector Church for its continued support and for helping me to hold onto my Christian values.

So much love to Deborah Johnson and Latisha Glover-Tate for always and continuously spreading my voice with others; Reginald T. & Truitt C. for your contribution & support; Odene Lewis for the great book review and excellent work she does; to all my friends who listened during the good and the bad; and my web designer, Kojo Tate (KFX Graphix). Much gratitude to Mystic Living Today for sharing my poetry with the online world.

Thanks to all who have supported my efforts and those who continually pass my inspirational words to others. I love receiving the notes, emails, and phone calls that let me know how my expressions may have had an impact on lives. One of the greater joys of writing is when it touches someone else and when taking a part of what I do improves or inspires someone else. I will always have a continued connection and passion for not just wanting but needing to help people out of genuine love.

My Pen Speaks

Poetic Mind Vibes

Project Rebound

Project Rebound is an organization
With a huge plan to move forward
To recoil from turmoil
To recover and discover
New ways to encourage our people
To bounce back from deceitful attacks
To rebuild a legacy that has already begun
To persevere without fear
To give laughter, project rebound has
Always shown great character.
Project Rebound continues commemorative celebrations for
    freedom
Freedom that pushes self determination and dedication
Freedom for equal justice of all people
Freedom for peace in our hearts.
Celebrating throughout the years
Learning from others how to persevere.
Celebrating independence, slavery, rebuilding lives and
    cultural principles,
Letting the world see we're not invincible.
Project Rebound has brought to the forefront renown historians,
To give us knowledge of our past Victorians,
And how we began our victorious journey.
Our leaders have motivated our spiritual souls,
And empowered us to take hold, to be multicultural and multiracial
In order to bring living peace within us
To show that a higher power makes the call for us all.
They have a commitment to social and economic development
To continue to rebuild an unforgettable legacy.
Project Rebound is an organization built on a firm foundation
Giving back to the community
In order to celebrate all of life's seasons.

*"Project Rebound is a profound organization that will be
around for many generations to come"*   Columbus, GA

A New Drug

A new drug
An ultimate healer
Not a pass-me-by drug dealer,
A lover of all things
Not one that helps us fall to our knees,
One that grants me peace
Not one that may cause my last breath
And bring me to my death,
He died on the cross to pay for our sins
Let's repay him and obey him with a new beginning
Have faith, seek him within,
Don't inhale, but exhale and feel
The true power of his love
Let's become addicted to a new drug.

A Plea to a Friend

Things happen to us
we have no idea why
situations in our lives
we wonder why
situations are put upon us
why now, why this
be the example for someone else
create a new expression of attitude
be accepting of the path prepared for us
let go and allow him to have his way
we struggle from day to day
but it's not our battle
we usually know the right things to do
though others may not jump to your rescue
don't allow yourself to stoop to their level
though the devil is busy
and temptation gets in your way
if in fact this does happen
ask him for forgiveness
He never stops watching
He never stops listening.

And neither do I. . . .

As I Dreamed a Vision into Reality

Fighting battles, but not beyond endurance
The risk of dreaming dreams no one could see but me.
Reaching above my own expectations
To accomplish the unknown.
No tears flowing, because I'm no longer at a standstill
Accepting the things that I cannot change.
During challenging times
And no support to motivate my efforts
Often contemplating not dreaming at all
But my visions wouldn't allow anything less.
Slipping a few times and falling short
While striving to climb the ladder
Knowing the end result is what really mattered.
Trying not to complain but taking action
For the satisfaction I wanted in my life,
As I dreamed, my picture became clearer
No longer just visualization
But dreams of my life's reality
As I continue to reach for the rainbows
In hopes of touching the stars!!!

Back on Track

Changing the right images
In your mind's eye
Don't be trapped
Snap out of it, it's over
Discover something different
Fall into a state of euphoria
In the beginning it didn't make sense
Until you created something new
Bigger and better things
Processing the old melancholy
We understand you fell out of the loop
For a minute but now you're back in it
To stay on track
To boost your life
With a phenomenal impact.

Changing Life

Jesus Christ should be blowing our minds
He is the greatest thing in our lives
He shed his blood for us all
He loves us all, completely
You should be singing glory, glory
But that's another story you have yet to grasp.
There are seeds of greatness buried inside you
You must learn to share them in all that you do.
If you love the Lord don't let him go,
Let him know.
Stop feeding your insecurities
By indulging in the power of your attitude
Make a choice to stay focused
By building your support and
Leaning on family and friends for reinforcement.

Charity

From the moment your bright smile entered the room
My prayer was that you truly knew what you were doing.
Your confidence was well noted.
I'm sure when entering a new patient's room
You're probably a little reserved,
Not knowing the person's mood.
As time progressed we conversed more
Which made me that much more comfortable
Each time you walked through the door.
As we talked about the word just
And being who we are
We are just many things but never
Less than what God wants us to be
But much more because he foresees,
You will be what he has destined for you.
From birth he had a plan for Charity
It's just sometimes we need that clarity.
Just hold onto your faith
And allow him the space
To plant your seed on solid ground,
Continue to listen to the sound of his voice
He always gives you that choice.
Your name is a part of who you are
And who you will become,
To give to this world
As much as you can
By caring and giving and assisting others.
To continue living
To encourage those who may have given up on life
Letting them know there is much strife
But if it's God we trust, then it's worth fighting for
The more you give of self,
The more you will receive
From Charity....

Dedicated to Charity (nurse at Wellstar Cobb Hospital)

Favor in My Father's Eyes

Favor in my Father's eyes
Where He can see all
And we're blinded by lack of faith
Favor in my Father's eyes
Saving our souls from the
Webs of demons
Keeping His eye on the sparrow
As He protects His lost children
He pleads with us to be in the likeness of Him
For He sees our path and has paved the way
We are beginning to see the sunrise
A new day is dawning
He has brought forth new meaning to life
We've been taught to look before we walk
To think before we speak
To pray before we weaken
Yet we still fall
But He's always there demonstrating his power
To lead us to the righteous path
In order to walk into his home called Heaven
Favor in our Father's eyes
He continues to speak to us
Because he knows the devil
Will try to control our soul
Favor in my Father's eyes
We are his children
Never to forget He has all power and control
He keeps us in his heart forever.

Feeling His Presence

Feeling His presence is only the
    Beginning of your many blessings

  To ignore him would be one of
    Your many downfalls

    Serve him by reading his word
      Helping others to say the least

      He's watching you
        Hear him

        He's showing you the way
          Walk into his light. . . .

Artificial Tears

My artificial tears flow on the inside
Masking my fears of the life before me
Waiting to fly free
Looking for the 'me' that used to be
Free-spirited.

Pausing for a moment to see the dawn
Anticipating the new sunrise
Wishing for something new and true
Blue skies and clear ocean waves
Longing to see these visions
Become my truth, my life, my earth's fruit.

The hourglass is nearing its end
What will happen at that time remains to be seen
A clear mind, a clear heart, no hesitation in sight
Waiting for a long time, not allowing the
Longevity to seize love from my soul.

The madness that life's relationships put us through
The calm that love brings us to
Is the ultimate satisfaction
Leaving fewer tears, fewer fears
Of love and the lack of artificial tears.

He Keeps on Loving Me

He keeps on loving me
Though I've sinned again and again
He gives me the glory
Even when I don't listen
He keeps on loving me
Though the storms continue
Eternally I can depend on him
He keeps on loving me
He always gives me a resting place
Not allowing me to fall flat on my face
What more can I ask for
Than a heart that's divine
Always knowing more blessings
For me are next in line.
Through trying times
I may have felt he wasn't giving me
All that I needed, but yet
He keeps on loving me.

He's Waiting

Beyond a lifetime of listening
Time and time again answering our prayers ...
We all have a projected movie of the ideal life for us,
And all of its pleasantries.
As well as life, death should also be pleasant.
It's the transition that's difficult for us all.

The weapons of war and mass destruction impacting so many
    lives,
We never know how it may come at us.
We have all been hurt by love or lack of it in this world.
Remember to release and let go. Remember how to love and
    allow love in.
Know that not all are of an evil and mean spirit.
Through prayer we can diminish, endure, heal and rise above
    all.
So regardless of what you've seen or heard,
God has the final word. HE IS THE VICTORY!!!

Land of Hope

In the land of hope my tent is sturdy
And my time is just one step ahead
My vision is clear
My eyes are no longer weeping in sorrow
But the tears of joy have begun to flow
Sometimes we feel so down
Sometimes we see no tomorrow
Ask anything in His name and He shall give it.
Listen and use these words in prayer
Tell him exactly what you need
He is your sword, your rock and your shield
No man can do what he does
In the land of hope
Extend your faith
Just pray!!!

Broken Hearts, Shattered Pieces

When you're done
  Lashing out, cry out
When you're done
  Cursing out, forgive without a doubt
When you're done
  Beating yourself up, let go, let up
When you're done
  Allowing any one person to mold and change who you become
    Show them what's been instilled in you and where
      you come from
Be the person to break away from the restraint
  Give it to God with no complaints
    Forgive but never forget, because you never want to
      backtrack
When you're done
  With self doubt and clouding your own way
    Pick yourself up and find your way
      Back into a life of second chances
        Understanding that God is with you
          But you also have to be demanding
Though this may seem impossible to achieve
  The creator has given you strength to believe
To live your life as it was intended
  Open up your heart, never pretending
    Knowing its okay to love again. . . .

Light of Darkness

The light of darkness
Usually protrudes through
Our wounded souls.
Even though we try to mask
The drama in our existence.
The discretion of our grace
Falling upon one's face.
The path of righteousness
We want so, to lead, but astray
We're driven to proceed.
The darkest days by night
Were one after the other
But the sweetest dawn will rise
When you least expect it
My heart is so excited
Its broken valves are reconnecting
As he continues to bless me.

God's Miracles

God's creations are a mystery of the mind
We often wonder how and why he's always on time,
But if we keep the faith and keep on believing in him
He will deliver, he will never leave you out on a limb.

If we keep the faith we'll continue to receive
His many blessings, deliverance he does achieve.
God's miracles, he keeps on bringing
God's miracles, let's keep on singing,
About the great blessings we have received
About the many accomplishments we have achieved.

The creator of all things, through our being
He delivers things he has already foreseen
Blessings you never before imagined nor dreamed of,
But through God's miracles, from heaven above
He is our redeemer.

Through God's miracles he delivers life,
He delivers us from strife.
He'll lift you up, when darkness falls,
Nothing too tough, just pray and give God a call.
Lifting your spirits to new heights
Never failing to show you there is a brighter light.

Life's True Satisfaction

Stumbling along life's course
Having an uncommon wisdom of life
If you have fallen
The lesson is not to collapse
In the same trench
But to fill it with faith
And never have to
Fill it again.
But to replenish it with gained strength
We all have limitations
But despite our limitations
We find our strengths and focus.
Spinning the wheel that was never turning,
Always some unclear thoughts of the future,
But our desire for life should have grown deeper
No need to indulge ourselves in
The increasing assets
That we acquire, but the investment
And enrichment we have
Through God which is true satisfaction
Praise should be the way
In which we say
Thank you, Jesus!

From a Poet to God

What does it take to make it through
The road to you
Not that I'm ready for you
I just have so much love for you
So much more to give to the world
For you.

What does it take to be true to you
To be in the stars with you
Not that I'm ready for you
Just wanna be sure I get to you
Just wanna hold onto you
Not that I'm ready for you
Just wanna spread love for you
Give my world to you.

I just can't stop living for you....

Faith As I Pray

Give me faith
As I pray to you today
As I am able to do your will
Give me the strength to give and forgive
Give me faith as I pray.

Continue to allow me to walk and speak
On the trails of deliverance when I fall weak
No one else can do these things
No one else can grant me the blessings you bring
Healing hearts that are on bended knees
Give me faith as I pray.

Healing hearts that are on bended knees
Believing you're the one who can truly see
Praying continually that you know that I believe
As I patiently await you to see me through
My faith will continue to be in you
Give me faith as I pray.

Confused....

Confused
About my next move
Don't wanna loose
Necessary to lead the life I choose
Don't wanna loose
Myself, my goals, my purpose
Don't wanna loose
The balance, super fast or super slow
Something in between to enhance my growth
Don't wanna loose
The cells in my battery
The gauge is low
And needs recharging
Don't wanna loose my sparkle
Twinkle, twinkle there is no star
Therefore I need to bring my life up to par
Don't wanna give in to control
Makes me sour and bitter to the taste
Evolving to a better place
While I run this race
Trusting someone with my life
Is where I wanna start
My heart is where I wanna be
The smart thing to do is trust and be true
Don't wanna deprive myself of anything
Everything to give
And so much to live for
Taking the possibilities to achieve more
So anxious and incomplete
About my next move
Definite plans I don't wanna loose
Refusing to settle for less, no longer Confused....

Random Hearts

Random hearts connecting inconspicuously
Strangers by day acquainted in their distance
Innocence of the mind
Accountable to the eye
Culprits together
Even as they live alone
Theatre of the mind
As they act out
Becoming complicated
The center of drama
In their small world that used to be peaceful
Trying to overcome the optimistic ending
To a short-lived association
As they came to a heartfelt realization
That they're composite and structure
Would never mesh as one.

One Love

Loving one like no other
Loving one heart to another
Conceiving true love can only live for one soul
Achieving true love is one's definitive goal
Surrendering all is that binding connection
To the success of true love and ambient affection
Sharing this with no intrusions
Confusing this by permitting infusion
Would be crushing to the transparency promised
Hesitant to giving of oneself completely and whole heartedly
Investing in love keeps the mind strong
Continuous love for the long haul
Not infatuation but pure admiration
Willingness to reveal, accept, and give freely
Vulnerability at your feet
Accepting you as the love for my heart only
No more loneliness just pure bliss in the midst of it all
All yours or not at all
Here's my heart, it's your call.

I Can't Breathe

Rescue me I can't breathe
Give me light to see a clearer path
My light is dim I can no longer see through the fog
My voice is faint from the screaming echoes of my own voice
My pace is slower because I've been dragging my feet to my
    own destiny
My fingers are numb from the bondage of an unclear mind
That won't allow my pen to speak
Rescue me so that I may prosper
Give me light to continue my journey
Give me a voice so I can speak poetically
Give me a steady walk to perseverance
Release the blood that needs to run through my veins
To allow me to release the most powerful words my mind has
    ever imagined
My mind, body, and soul needs the earth's soil to grow my
    wings
As I crawl out of my caterpillar skin into a vibrant butterfly.

Habitual Love

What should be the height of his life
At the bottom he stood
Contemplating settling for misery for the remainder of his life.
There was no other that he wanted in his existence
Until his determination became persistent.
A connection to the missing link was made
Though not a free and clear connection
But one of a mutual mindset.
Not wanting to be stuck in a lost world of unhappiness
United but still lonely
Knowing life at its present state
Was no longer recoverable
One not willing to make the sacrifices in life to save the
    promise
To cherish life as one together
Hearts torn in many directions
Will he go another century waiting to be loved completely?
Continuing to search his heart's desires
Anticipating his future endeavors of life's true satisfaction of
    love,
Or will he continue to live in habitual love?

Live, Love, Laugh

Happy beginnings don't always remain
Sad endings sometimes stay the same
Even in the midst of turning things around
Life gets confusing and even amusing
New beginnings of living, loving, and laughing
Should be our focus to get to prosperity and lifelong dreams.
Life is full of mystery and predictions
But life is what you make it despite all obstacles.
Naturally we have anxiety, but He tells you
If you take one step, I'll take two,
In order to get you to your destiny.
The destiny He designed for you, the one you've allowed

Many trials to slow your pace
But He has always kept you in His grace.
He wants you to achieve, so try to repay Him
By putting your fears aside and put your
Faith in place.
Believe in Him as you say you do.
Show him you trust Him to deliver what He has in store
Show Him you trust Him to open that other door.
Don't block your blessing by being afraid to live out His will.
Sometimes life has its way of changing our direction
But just relax, because He has the map to put you back on track.
Live your life to the fullest, because life is too short
To live it any other way,
Pray to Him each and everyday
And He will restore your life
Today!

Positive Living

Positive living
Leads to inspirational giving,
Assisting others
In how to discover
The significance of God's power.
When you awake in the morning
To take another step into life's journey,
Live as if you know he's watching
Do something to make him proud
Something as simple as praying out loud.
Serve him and be giving of yourself
Have purpose, not strife, stay steadfast
And he will reward you with
A purpose-driven life.
When your mind is on that road
Traveling through a negative mode,
Stand up and take notice
Christ is our Lord and Savior
Thank him by being devoted.
Begin to exhale
Hold on to your faith and trust in him too,
And give praise for what he has already given you.
We're all guilty of some form of sin,
But that's no reason to continue down
That spiraling dead end,
By extending the welcoming hand of the devil,
But instead pull together, pray together, stay together
By serving Christ
And begin to enjoy the true
Meaning and gift of life.

Pride, Determination, and Resilience

We live our lives in hopes of leaving some mark on the world
We live our lives in hopes of making someone feel something
We live our lives in hopes that our efforts won't go unnoticed.

You and I against all odds
Making a change to enhance the livelihood of others
No doubt of our motives
Inner city children overlooked
And living in poverty,
But hold the key to sovereignty.
Hopeful of life's many opportunities
Taught to never give up
And continue striving to the top.
Pride won't allow them to fail
Determination drives them to go the distance
Resilience keeps them grounded
And promises perseverance.

Strike Back

How do we react
To hostile criticism
We usually strike back
But that's natural to react
But learn to smile and accept
Your challenges
When someone means you harm
Remove yourself
Deal with them in harmony
Not stooping to their level
Of torment, imitating the devil.
Pray for their mishaps
And perhaps you will be blessed
And no longer in distress.
Never get accustomed to the abuse
Lay it on the line
Allow him to deal with them
In his own time.

Taking My Life Back

I've allowed you to chip and nip
And tarnish my soul for far too long.
I know I was taught long ago to pray
And hold steadfast, stay strong
And give my battles to God.
What really happened in between that,
I can't even begin to explain,
But now has come the time to reconstruct
You see you can't hold me down
For eternity unless I allow you to,
But you already know he has given me the
Strength to rejoice and renew.
I've asked him to cleanse my soul
And take control of his child.
To guide me back on track,
To give me courage to never allow you to attack
My character again, but to build it.
To give me knowledge to shape and mold my children to
Follow his grace. From this moment on there is no lack of faith
From this moment on I'm taking my life back....

The Binding

The binding that ties us
together as a people
are the words we speak
and the life we commit to
that is made possible
through Christ.

As it has been stated, that a
man's word is his bond,
and if he has no words
then what is his bond?

a simple thought. . . .

Thank You! Thank You!

Thank you, Thank you!
For the glimmer of light even in total darkness.

Thank you, Thank you!
For the pain, so that I could see the sunlight and rain.

Thank you, Thank you!
For kneeling closer to thee, so that I could see the beautiful
    qualities inside of me.

Thank you, Thank you!
For giving me a gift to pen this paper, so I could shift my life
In another gear to an end result that is clutter free, crisp and
    clear.

Thank you, Thank you!
For opening my eyes so that I could see far beyond the years
    that had just passed me by.
Most good but the bad tried to keep me there to die
A torn soul, half and half, no control.

Thank you, Thank you!
For the extended hands that commanded me to stand up
And land on sturdy foundation to plant seeds for the next
    generation.

Thank you, Thank you!
For testing me, Thank you for blessing me, thank you forever
    and ever continuously, Thank you!

Search for Love

They don't want to be the one's dying inside
So they have to be the ones who live
Through a mounting relationship
Though others are falling apart
Trying to manage the best they can
Knowing their next move may be morally mistaken
Feelings of compassion and companionship emotionally true
Who holds the key to this puzzle
Who will connect the dots
Is it safe to say they truly care
Or is it for one eye only
Though they feel they know the heart's connection
Still so afraid of the unknown
That could cut deep and cause a bleeding heart
That could grasp deep and cause a rhythmic heart
To skip with joy
Patiently awaiting the sunset
Though not knowing whether it's next rise
Will shine upon the other
The search for love has finally and morally met its match…

When Nothing Changes

When nothing changes for the better,
Do something different,
When there are no positive results
Restructure your strategies to do good will.
Follow Christ and delegate to your disciples.
Reach out to people in several ways.
Focus on all aspects of serving others.
Explore the gifts you've been given to
Connect with others. BE THE LIGHT FOR
Someone else's darkness…

The Real "F" Word—FORGIVE

Forgive me for I have sinned
As you wipe my slate again and again
With an humble heart and much regret
These are the days I shall repent.
Forgive me when I'm weak, when I fail
Pray that my sins aren't leading me to a jail cell.
When times are of despair and I ponder my rescue
Lead me to have faith and depend on you.
Forgive me as I live and discover
Forgive me as I make my mistakes
And pave an example for another.
Some days are short and simple
Others are strenuous and hard,
But I know you're in my corner for the duration
And the end of that road, it's you at my celebration.
As I've turned the right left
And gone the distance,
And made my way into your existence
In hopes of passing your test
Keeping away from damnation and
Walking into the throne of salvation.

Food for Your Soul

Today do good deeds surprise the unexpected
Inspire someone who might be socially rejected or
    disconnected…
Give someone a hug
Rather than a shoulder shrug…
Be the leader of the pack
You may help someone get back on track…
Be happy with no complaints…
Smile at someone who's frowning
You never know they might be drowning…
Bless someone because you have been blessed…
Know that someday someone will return the favor…

GBG Reloaded

GBG

Grafted by Grace

A group of men grafted by grace
Linked together to spread God's
Love and tender embrace
Playing and singing songs of rejoice
Music with a mission and a voice by choice
Believing that God is to be honored, respected,
Praised and celebrated.
Since they can't be all over the world
Hopefully their message will, through
One boy one girl
One day at a time.
It's not by chance that they all have connected
They are the chosen few that were selected
And by his grace we will never forget
How they've already touched so many souls
In their ministry of music and testimonials
They are prepared mentally and physically with no fear
Outstanding they are and commanding your attention
They are united and truly still standing!

Doing God's Work!!!

War, Pain, and Deadly Sacrifice

Battling their peers
Trying to refrain from fear
Soldiers full of courage
To defend their country.
Fighting for rights
Rights even they have no idea about
Issues of world politics.
Weapons of war
Assembled for major destruction
Going through personal turmoil
To be loyal
To a world full of hate
Not willing to join together
Not even for Jesus Christ's sake.
Witnessing brutal death
And devastating health.
Raging battlefields
Where opponents will never yield,
To save the lives of their
Women and children, allowing them to live.
Men and women of war
Taking the risk of returning alive
Or ending up in war's personal archive.
Returning home in a body bag
To be buried beneath their country's flag.
Tears of hurt and pain
The soldiers have to sustain
Heart-wrenching pain
The sight of unimaginable death
Impacting so many lives
From the torment of war's destruction.
But in the end God has the final word
So regardless of what you've seen or heard
HE IS THE VICTORY!!!

Music

Music is water for the soul
drink it up,
it moves you
causing your soul to erupt.
Music is an incision
that heals open wounds
feeling the melodies from every tune.
Music is passion
passion like soft kisses.
Music is listening to the rain
hitting the window pane,
while reminiscing down memory lane.
Music is crucial keys
touched by magical hands,
it's love, love of bass, drums, and tenor
and every instrumental.

Music soothes the soul
it releases your mind
reaching, grabbing hold
like you're reaching for gold,
feeling the weakness from songs of love
that make you speechless
putting you in a trance
that's so intoxicating,
like making love
it's so amazing.

Music gets you high on life
so relaxing, you forget life's strife.
Music is food for the soul
feels as if you're in total control.
Music is attitude
a whole new magnitude.
Music is my calm during the storm
makes your heart melt, feeling warm.
Music can bring the world together
through each and every endeavor,
Music is an expression
that has often taught us a lesson
of patience and unimaginable experiences,
learning not to complain but to sustain
the trials and tribulations
to take action to gain satisfaction.
Music is sitting in the rain
not knowing you're getting wet
soothing, like watching the sun set.
Indulge yourself in music
watch the magic
it's our paradise.

Keep It Simple

Naturally complicated
But simply stated
God has laid it out on the pages
But we misinterpret it
And pave it out in our own stages.

Free yourself

And gain contentment in knowing
Loving God, loving others, serving God
And serving the world is simply stated
But we create the natural complications
Simplify by reconstructing your train of thought
Realizing that everything you've been taught
Is not set in stone.

Accept the facts

You've been given a common knowledge
To know the difference between right and wrong
Use what you know for certain to hold faith
In the palm of your hand and take a stand
Be a leader as one of his disciples and lead strong.

A Mother's Love

No love like a mother's love,
No stronger bond on earth.
The precious bond that comes from God
A spirit so sweet, mild and unique.
A mother's love is forever strong,
Love spread in just the right measure,
Love you'll forever treasure.
Love designed
To lift our wings and define our destiny.
To have and to hold her husband
To prepare and mold her children
Almost never given a woman's worth
While here on earth.
Her love lives on even
When her days on earth are over
Through generations
With God's blessing hands on each one.
Loving with emotional connections
From the influence God has given,
Love rising
Above and beyond
To an unconditional mother's love.

A Silent Connection

Doing all that we do
Maintaining our sanity
Needing to get away
Taking time out for us
Daydream the dream
Floating out to sea
Blue skies just you and me
Gazing at the silent night sky
Stealing away a kiss
Hearing the noiseless air
Amazing it is
The comfort of
The oceans waves
Arms intertwined together
Our voices uttering not a word
Still in time
Knowing we're at peace
Looking, listening, speaking no words
But hearing everything.
We are connected...silently.

Communicating with TLC

Expressing our needs is easier said than done.
How to do this with tender love
Not embarking on the small things
Trying to focus on living, loving, and being happy
Wanting it more than anything
Trying to get that across without
Saying those direct words
Praying our indications and needs are heard
Our hearts are more delicate than we wish to admit
We play the low key everyday
But our eyes try to stroke them with an intense glare
We know we both have it but why is it suppressed
How do we release it before we're all depressed?
Love is like the sun setting only to rise again, stronger
With each setting, with beaming bright shimmers of light
That sets near dawn with a calming glow
Like love you always remember it having its special place
Holding on intensely, releasing the tenderness throughout
The remainder of our lives together
With us both having the same purpose in life,
To love and to be loved....

Expressions, Perception, and Stamina

It's all about our expressions.
How we withstand, what's your perception.
We've been through a lot together
Through all the stormy weather
We can't retract the stormy nights
But we can open up to brighter days and nights.
You're my only love, for eternity
You've accepted me as I have you.
Through the good, the bad
The joys and sorrows, the new, the you.
As you know, it's you I adore
And because I love you for who you are
Even the corny things make me love you that much more.
All times are critical in our lives
Not caring about the other one's needs
Only leads to division and separation proceeds.
If you still choose me first, say what you must
Show me your love, show me your thirst.
It's all about the stamina, we've held steadfast
And shared our love.
There is no perfect being, but with each other
We have shown feelings of comfort together
Feelings of protection, through any storm
Through any kind of weather.

Love at the Bayou

Sitting at the edge of the lake
He began to wash my feet
Continuing our journey
Watching the sun set
Beautiful warm tones
Disappear right before our eyes
Lying in the field of grass
Watching airplanes fly over
Imagining walking on the clouds
Leaving our footprints in mid air
Posting our love across the sky
How could passion reach such a high?
Subtle symbols of love, yet deep
Watching wild flowers
And windmills blowing
Miles of road ahead
We were connected
Yet tangible and free
We were extraordinary as individuals
And gallantly unique together
Needing each other at that very moment
Superceding every negative emotion
From our past thoughts
Our faces are like mirrors
When we look at the other
Smiles gleaming
Even though the sun had faded
Our hearts were full
But continuously making
Room for our love.

Loves of My Life

The loves of my life
Entered this world through my very being
With the miracle of God, foreseeing.
Birth I was able to give
And allow two beautiful children to live.
Not only once, but twice
He allowed me to give life.
When they entered this world
I was filled with joy,
The first love of my life was a baby boy.
Two years later came a little girl,
Both a bundle of love, a jewel, a pearl.
When you give birth, they say you should bond,
But the bond is already there, like a ray of sun.
I looked into their eyes
I could already feel the ties,
That bond parent and child
Pleasantly calm and mild.
Bundles of joy all wrapped in their blankets
Watching them gaze around, looking for familiarity,
Soon to be sure to see you with clarity.
Remembering the pain you thought, unbearable.
Looks of innocence and unconditional love,
A gift of love that you know
Could only have come from God above.

to my children—Bobby & Akieria Hall

My Brother, My Son

My son, my protector, my omega man
You've upheld every mother's demand,
You've made me proud
In every way that you can.
When I look at you, I see your father
A mirrored image of my hero,
Shining through the years
I've watched you grow.
Remembering when your father
Passed away to a better place,
I picture the smile on his face,
As he watches over this joyous occasion.
The painful feelings we still feel,
When we think of him, heart wrenching and real.
Feelings of despair, you can't compare.
But we must remember it's best
And his soul is at rest.
You don't remember your father's request
As a little boy, putting your manhood to the test.
Requesting of you to take care of your sister and me,
And of his wish, you have certainly kept complete.
Now you've begun another era in your life,
You've bonded with your beautiful wife.
Lovable she is with a voice of grace,
That you fell in love with, everyone can see it in your face.
Two families have met and joined as one,
In God's place of grace,
You'll both keep a heavenly bond.
Inspired by (Mrs. Maddox) a mother's love…

Overlooked

She was always there overlooked by his gaze
But something opened his eyes
And once again she was there
Now he has the peace of knowing he is loved
So much good has come his way
Since she came into his life
He knows that he can't let anyone
Take that away.

His future isn't the same
She took his heart
She keeps taking him higher
In the beginning he was looking for love
And she amazed him with such
He was lost and she helped him find
His way back into her life, God's way.

Removing the Mask

Removing the mask
revealing the depth of your soul
begin to grasp life
taking responsibility and control
of life's direction.

Let's stop pretending and sweeping
the dust to mix with the
air in which we breathe.

The feeling of imagining it will
all dissipate
don't be deceived, do something
before it's too late.

What we're feeling is evident
in action
floating through daily routine
and everyday distractions,
not attempting to bring our
lives its deserving satisfaction.

Both knowing through the storms
our hearts should keep the other warm.
This time be wise
open up your eyes
don't be afraid to disrupt
your schedule
removing the mask
ceasing to cover up
appreciating what we have
understanding what we share
moving in the direction
of a fulfilling life
wanting to cherish the bond
between husband and wife.

Rhythm of the Universe

The rhythm of the universe, it's happening, I'm taking a
    chance
But afraid at the same time, stepping out, stepping up-
Life is waiting, but not, I've waited for this moment
To share my space, though still reserved, just in case
Heart pulsating from anticipation, knowing you're open for my
    air
To breathe in yours, the manner in which I move
When your presence appears, when you touch my face, gently
While our eyes are gazed upon the other, we drift into our aura
Some time has passed, and we've continued our path
Now I know why true love lasts, because we're the rhythm of
    the universe.

Sisters and Friends, for Life, Forever

The sound of chatter
From sisters enjoying each other's company,
The love spread over the years
Helping one another conquer our fears.
As we began to share our dreams
Planning for your children
That I love as my own
We both admire how they have grown.
Feeling great pleasure
From their bubbly smiles
And innocent eyes,
The energy and spunk, so alive
Hearts breaking once again
As we see their sorrow,
Knowing their mother was hurting,
As we ask God to deliver you
To allow you to see your children blossom,
For they are our dreams of tomorrow.
Through this unexpected attack on life
Accompanied by your crisis,
The pain in their hearts
We had never imagined possible
Praying daily for you to recover
From this disaster that had been discovered.
The pain begins
But seemed to never end,
Even with the problems we've had
Our hearts have come together,
As sisters, friends, for life, forever.
Reminiscing the simple joys of life,
Forgiving the past
And looking forward to the future,
Late night talks on the phone
Awaiting my next visit to your home.
Saying things we never meant,

Knowing that agreeing on everything is impossible
As we are all created to be different.
Hoping for the strength
To endure these obstacles,
Obstacles that help build our faith
In order to stay in God's grace.
Sister and friend I say to you
I pray for you and all that you do.
We can't allow life to pass us by,
So let's capture all the love and joy,
That God has planned for us.
In him we must love and trust,
He has given us a new beginning
For our hearts to share together,
Sister and friends, for life, forever.

So Amazing

No words could express how I felt
As I embraced you with so much love.
We watched your glowing brown eyes
As emotions passed through with each stare.
Anticipating every move, every sound you made
Each one more exciting than the previous
You brightened each and every day.
We often search for true love
And rarely do we sustain it
But the joys we get from our children
Is the true love we search for every day.
Storing each moment in our hearts forever
Awaiting the memories to come.
As your father and I turned the pages
To figure out our next phase in life
You were growing, developing and
Moving around, kicking, turning, stretching,

Developing into your own being, already full
Of energy, showing us that you
Would be a major part of our future.
All taking place within my body as
One of the most amazing experiences in existence.
I knew your life would be in my hands
And you would be one of our greatest joys.
I've been in love like this before
Each one different from the other
And it's pure joy this time as well.
I'm happy God chose to allow you
To come to be, through me
I pray about all the things that will
Come from your existence.
As we began to choose names for you
Wanting that to be a perfect
Combination with your personality
A spiritual joy you've already come to be.
Hoping to instill in you to never
Stray from your faith and
To always remember you have a
Special place in our hearts.
It has to be a great feeling to
Be wanted and loved by so many people.
True blessings as you enter into your new world
To be loved abundantly.

Special One

She's feisty as fire
But still of a sweet spirit
Shows great demonstration
And character of her life's desires
She has many genuine talents
To demonstrate as she contributes
Sunlight into someone else's life
What she gives isn't always what she receives
But she continues to be generous in good faith
And has gained God's respect
Times have certainly changed
And values are different
But her value is sacred and unchangeable
Strong bonds in marriage, friendship, church life
And relationships are key pieces of life
We often go without expressing our love
But sometimes the unspoken words
With outward gestures of love are just as valuable.
As we are all created to be different
And have every reason to celebrate life's seasons
Reminiscing and delighting
Yourself to the simple joys of life
Special One I say to you
That we pray for you and all you do
We won't allow life to pass us by without
Giving you the love and recognition you deserve.

Congratulations on your retirement-Aunt Carrie Williams

The Love for Me

The love for me
that God has sent back into my life.
He to be my husband
and I to be his wife.
A picture not of perfection
but of the love we share
to bring the other happiness
and a love bond beyond compare.
Nothing is ever promised to us,
however, Gods hands have been
laid upon us,
and in him we must trust.
When flowers bloom
I'm reminded of how we have grown.
When I awake to the sun shining bright,
I'm reminded of his smile,
The glow I see in his eyes
when reminiscing about our unborn child.
Throughout this life we will have
joy and sorrow and tears from both,
but as long as we're together united as one,
we can handle life's challenges as they come.
He could have chosen differently
but chose to have me in his heart,
to share our united front.
I could have chosen differently
But felt as if God brought us
together to never part.
What seems like a miracle in itself
to experience life unfolding
to a true and gracious ending,
only to introduce a new beginning,
of an extended family joined as one
to forever be inseparable.

True to Self

Some time has passed since I saw you last
Not knowing how you would receive me
Or the things I wanted to say to you
Those apprehensions I put aside
To express the feelings I've kept inside.

You said yes to the question, me asking to see you
I had no expectations of what would come of it, if anything
But, I was prepared for the worse
The worse being, the beginning of our end.

He knows the one my heart longs for
He introduced us several years ago
You are everything I believed Him for
You are the one I passion for.

I give all my love and heart to you
I want to earn your trust and love again
By being true to self and telling you
…… I'm in love with you

by J.A. Williams

Untitled

You were talked about without even knowing
Unaware of the people you would influence
Unknowing of their motives
Oblivious to how you would be received
I was told of your expected arrival
By someone who spoke very highly of you
It helps that this someone is somewhat a mutual friend to us
    both
Giving us a connection for our first encounter.

As with most "first" meetings or introductions
One seeks to discover common interests about the other
As a means of easing the tension and anxiety
That unfortunately gets in the way of human relations.

However, I'm convinced that we will have an immediate
    connection
Drawn together by a commonality that will be inconceivable
Building on a relationship that shall be indestructible
Unyielding to life's harms that are sure to confront us.

Today is the day of your scheduled arrival
Your arrival was moved up due to your apparent enthusiasm
My nervousness is said to be natural under the circumstances
As I'm about to witness first hand something truly amazing.

The mutual friend bringing us together is your mother
Whom you've gotten to know these past nine months
We have yet to meet but I am your father
As I count your ten fingers and toes, my beautiful baby girl.

by J. A. Williams

When It Rains, Come to Me...

When it rains, come to me, come to me, when it rains
Even in the midst of hail, come to me, when it rains
Seek the comfort, of love you know, not of false love
Some other being may attempt to show, through the storm
Allow me to calm your inner being, the way we talked about,
And vowed to sustain, come to me, when it rains
Straining to keep the rain at a minimal, let's slow our pace,
Allowing fate to erase hurt emotions, shifting our gear
In the right direction, so when I'm slightly distant, give me space
But not a hole to slip And fall into, and possibly get lost or drown
Let me know you're there, let me know you're around, at all
cost
Let's not get lost, in the heat of anger, acting like strangers
Putting our love in danger, right where it hurts the most
Allow me in to sooth your soul, we realize it only hurts
when it rains
And if we must let it rain, let it rain a cleansing stream,
so we can get back
on track, of our continuous dreams...TOGETHER....

Unforgettable

You're etched in my mind
Memoirs of your love painted over my heart
For my protection and symbol that we will never part
Thoughts of you with a delightful smile
Saying I see you well done my child
Knowing you're an angel of peace
Never ceasing to amaze me
Send me a sign
To ease my mind
As I build my trail
To leave my mark on life
As I calm the waters
And tip the scale
Not because I'm too heavy
But because I've climbed my way to higher ground
To encourage others and make you proud
I've begun to heal from the pain of you leaving
Though this type of pain will never completely fade
I'm content with that because I know you've created an
    amazing crusade
Of angels on high to show him you deserve his honor into heaven.

Man in the Mirror

You've grown in so many ways
But still needing to grow up
To begin your journey to manhood
I know it's hard and well understood
Because there was no real man to show you the way
But life has its way of placing you on that right road
To an open trail of positive life experiences
They often say that a mother can't raise her son to be a man
But I've done the best that I could do
But I know God has a master plan for you
My plea to you son is to remember Him well
And though you may continue to fall and stray
Admit your faulty mishaps and find your way
You hold a warm heart full of charm and charisma
See what I envision as the man in the mirror
Loving you with all my heart and soul
The pain of knowing all I can do is hope
That you were listening and pray that you gain control
Pray for your safety and shield of protection

I'll always be here with motherly love and affection
My heart bleeds with tears of pain
But I trust that my efforts aren't in vain
I believe in you when no one else will
So when you're feeling your life is at a standstill
Remember what you've been taught through the years
Open your heart and release your fears
I may not do all the things you want your way
But I'm always here to help you cross over into manhood
Just as any loving mother would.

Through My Eyes

Afraid of the unknown
And speaks out in a passive tone
She's one of my best friends
Meek and mild with slight attitude
Assertive in so many ways but all at the same time
Unassertive to conquer life
To reach for the stars
To leap into new beginnings and open new doors
A witty sense of humor
But afraid to soar
Refrains from making friends too quickly
And very selective in the process
If only she could see herself through my eyes
She would stop hiding behind that disguise
Her possibilities are great
Only if she would stop running attempting to escape
Build on what she has the power to change
To broaden her mind for a visual range
Build up her confidence
To begin her flight to success.

Some see her as quiet and shy
Part of this I can't deny
Some see her demeanor as lackluster and uncaring
But I challenge those to get to know her
And that perception would change for sure
Sure I'm her mother and a little biased
But I still challenge you to try it
True she's afraid to apply herself
And continues to keep her potential hidden inside
But as she lives and becomes more aware
Of how the world turns
Her creative juices will begin to churn
To others she's a teen not projecting
To me she's a beautiful young lady
And a blessing that I'll continue protecting
As I should.

A Letter from Mom

I envisioned the ultimate for you
Even before you made your grand entrance
I wanted you to have a perfect view of the world
I wanted everything around you to be pure and clean
Just as you would be.
You would be one of our greatest joys
You've already brought smiles to many faces
Even trying to pick a name for you
Was very difficult because we wanted
Your name befitting of your personality,
Your smile, and the character we would instill in you
As you grow into a woman.
My heart gets warm when I think of all
The people that are pleased about your arrival.

to my new addition-Zaire M. Williams

Love Me

Love me
The way that I love you
I wanna be a top priority
I wanna be the one that can
Never be removed from your heart
Comfort me when I'm down
Hold me until we both fall asleep
Make sure that I'm ok even when nothing is wrong
Consider me when you need to talk
Choose me when you feel there is no one to turn to
Love me
I wanna be the one you love endlessly....

Love Yourself

The need to be loved and accepted by others
The need to be loved and expressed from another
The need to be loved and judged by the world
We often compare ourselves to others
And criticize ourselves in the worse way
We pick ourselves apart
And feel worse than we did from the start
No need for this behavior
It's easier said than done
But if you can only hear these words
Then you've already begun
To heal and cease
Because you're the beauty in the beast
Repeat these words and begin to release
Leaving the attitude behind
It's all about your innertude
Find it in yourself and let it through
There is always someone prettier and smaller
There is always someone more handsome and taller
But you have to stand
And demand the love of self.

You Are!

You are the brightest star
You are the fullest moon
You are the highest cloud
You are the peak above all mountains.

When I hear your voice utter come as you are
I hear come in good spirit
Come with no spirit
Come with your heart
No matter how heavy
Come to be touched by healing hands
Not of man but by God's command.

Connecting the kids to the young adults
The young adults to the adults of wisdom
The adults of wisdom to wounded souls
The wounded soul to the broken hearted
The broken hearted to healing hands
Healing hands to touch lost souls
And all will connect to Jesus Christ!

No Father Without God

A father's love must have the guidance of God
To become a better man: a prominent man, not a dominant
    man.
A man has no true knowing of what it takes to give birth
But enough love to seek the knowledge and bring a child to
    this earth
As he admits his fears and seeks the knowledge
As he admits he's not there yet but willing to learn
Because of the feelings of being a good father, that he yearns.

A father's love must have the guidance of God
To show children parts of life that a mother can't
Children come into this world knowing close to nothing
They grow with lessons learned
A father teaches wrong from right and sometimes children will
    still stray
But a father's job is to continue to teach and pave the way

Children are of a free spirit and the key to our future
Teach them well and allow them to lead the way.

A father has to go to God, because He knows him, the man
    and who he is
And will guide him into his own
Time tells all but waits for no one
And a good father won't allow this time to pass him by
To miss out on raising a daughter or a son.
A father learns from the Father to never put life on a
    temporary hold
A father must take his family and seek God together,
In order to keep his family forever
If the pause button never gets pushed
He will miss the opportunity to really know God
A father's love was designed
To lift their wings and define their destiny.

The binding that ties us
together as a people
are the words we speak
and the life we commit to
that is made possible
through Christ.
So as he continues his journey
As a father to his son
Let not his bond be broken
But powerful words bonded as they are spoken.
Never fear the challenge, but tackle and defeat.
In order to take your seat, as the man, the father
Who holds the key
To a future that would not be.

A Man's Mind

You can't always read a man's mind
Doing all you can do to leave the blues behind
Trying to forget the lows
And embrace the highs
Igniting the desire to live as one
Challenging yourself to look inside your heart
Having the opportunity to live fulfilling lives
How can we catch our breath
When the air that we breathe is so thick
Wanting to make a change
To push harder for the stumbling blocks to be removed
When you run into dead ends
Turn around and go the other direction
Be honest in your quest
Because honesty must be the golden rule
To intertwine and digest a man's mind.

Caught by Storm

He knew nothing of her
Until the night before it all began.
His eyes caught her aura
As she walked through the automatic doors
His stare was evident but his words were not many
As he searched for them to part his lips,
Not to be boisterous but subtle in his approach.
As he spoke, not of many words but an introduction
Of himself. He was mesmerized by her eyes
And all else that his eyes could remember of her.
As she walked out of his sight, now knowing he
Might lay eyes upon her again
But still wondering would he part his lips
To ever speak words into her ears.
As time progressed the two became better
Acquainted. He came to know who she was

And what she represented. He was now more intrigued
And wanted to know more.
Only to find that she was already intertwined
With another, and he had no choice
But to withdraw his advances. All he could
Do was dream…Vanishing back into his normal world,
Never to return.…

Dreaming to Reality

As he tossed and turned restlessly
Uncontrollable pleasures began to creep into his mind
Her brown eyes, one of a kind
He could smell her aura, and hear her whispers
It all began with the two of them
Holding hands as they walked along the bayou
Forgetting their surroundings
While continuing endless conversation
Stopping at the perfect spot to sit and enjoy
The beautiful skies and the soft breeze that blew
Against their skin
For one moment in time they caught each other's stare
Their lips wanting to meet
So without hesitation, they moved forward into one another
A kiss of mutual passion
Lips of a perfect connection
They laugh a little because the wait was over
From what they both wanted and dared to say
Wanting actions to move forward
Without words
Encountering the perfect kiss
They then parted just long enough to
Prepare for a later date
She arrived to a sudden surprise of glistening candlelight
And nice chilled red wine and the dream goes on....

Dear Daddy,
With All Due Respect

Dear Daddy, with all due respect,
I'm feeling alone and full of neglect.
I'm supposed to feel love from my dear dad
But all I feel is angry, hurt and sad.
From the pain you've caused, I'm grieving
From what you've been doing, is so deceiving.
You brought me into this world to love and cherish me
But all you've done is left me with an open, bruised heart,
Mommy is continuously doing her part
Daddy, when are you planning to start.
I've loved you unconditionally
But you seem to stop loving me continually.
Our love is an uneven bond
A devil's web spun.
You should be the man I look up to
Daddy, give me joy, renew what you used to do.
Say goodbye to yesterday,
Start a new beginning
Start loving me today in every way.
Your dark world needs a ray of light
I'm praying that you dig deep in your soul
And find some insight.
Dear Daddy, with all due respect
I long to stop feeling unloved and full of neglect.

Inspired by little Miss Rice

Experience of Friendship

From first impressions others try to give
To closed eyes and how associates are revealed.
People infringing on how we perceive one another.
You and I not allowing that to happen,
Has grown into a meaningful friendship.
We've come from similar worlds
That the other can relate to.
Embarking on the unknown
Turning it into an experience to be remembered.
As we know friends don't always see eye to eye
They keep it real and learn not to lie
To one another, but sustain an open mind
To keep the friendship true, you know
The kind that's hard to find.
In our lifetime we have many dreams
And dreams aren't always what they seem,
But you are true to self, true to friends,
And true to life as you should be
And I appreciate you to the highest degree.

Love to one friend from another

Flags

The red flags are up
The white towel still hung
Around my neck
Yet I ponder and wait
I wonder and anticipate
The day we mesh as one
The way companionship was designed.
The moment we enter into
The comfort of the other
The days will grow stronger, better.
Not adhering to the realization
That time is of the essence.
Time tells all, but waits for no one.
We feel no pressure to please
Continuing a self-developing
Path of love or lack of.

Flirt

When
Love is a risky game
Be safe and just never call his name.
Have self confidence, show no shame,
When in doubt, just remember
They would do the same.

Mesmerize him with your eyes
But keep it real, never put on a disguise.
Minimizing yourself to some other kind
Of woman, he will visualize
As deceitful and full of lies.

When
Love becomes a risky game
Keep it simple so no one gets hurt,
Keeping him at a slight distance
But yet still have him craving for your dessert.
He will try to exercise his restraint
As you dress and enter the room, dressed to kill in your
Stiletto heels and short and sassy skirt
He'll crave you more…
Wanting to fall in love or maybe just score.
Not wanting either, you take a stand
Not wanting either, you take his hand
And head for the door.
Headed to your planned destination
Hitting the dance floor, dancing close.
Now he wants to hold you even more
Not wanting to intertwine
In the game of love,
Or his sexual fantasy
Continue to be true to self,
But at the same time
Keeping away from the triangle of madness.…

Floating Aimlessly

The man who doesn't really see you
When he's looking right at you
The man who wants you to cook and clean for him, And makes
sure he brings it to Your attention,
The man who has little romance in his rhythm
And knows it but does nothing to obtain it,
The man who satisfies part of you
But leaves the other unattended
He knows not what he has but longs to keep you near
The same man who does minimal for you but wants your all
The man who jumps to fulfill the needs
Of his peers, whether young or old
But doesn't have that same desire to Keep his promises to you
He wants you there for him
When he needs you and even when he doesn't
And even when he attempts to be there for you
He really isn't because his attention span has worn thin
Because of the others he's trying to leave a good
Impression upon,
But in the end what he's seeking from them will fade
And he'll come to you expecting for you to be
There waiting in the shade,
You're yearning for him, but he's away again
Not far, but seemingly thousands of miles away
You long for him to keep reaching out,
But he's infrequently focused long enough
To fulfill his true hearts desire.
Suddenly he remembers you,
He sees you still there but doesn't realize
A part of you is floating away…. Aimlessly.

Friend or Foe

Share good news
Support no matter what life I choose
Be happy when I prosper
Pick me up if I fall
Console me when I hurt from pain
Give me credit when I deserve it
Give me hell when I'm being a hypocrite
When I'm wrong voice your opinion
When I'm right accept the truth
When I stray give me a reality check
When I'm being put down defend my honor
When I need a hand, give me two
As a true friend, I'll do the same for you
Agreeing on everything is impossible
As we are all created to be different
But in determining friend or foe
Look, search deep in your heart
To reveal friend or foe
Surely time doesn't talk
But it tells everything
And sooner or later
It will reveal
Friend or foe.

From Rags to Riches

From rags to riches
And any kind of britches
From rags to riches
Even the wool kind that itches.
From no name
To brand name
From perfume Chloe
To J Lo's Glow
From pleather purses
To Louis Vuitton and Gucci clutches
Things we never knew of
Things we've begun to love
From taking Marta, where it's smarta
To drive it yourself, leave when you wanna.
From worn shoes
To Sean John and Air Force One's

What some will do for the Gucci shoe?
Or the designer bag that has become a part
Of the new fad
Like the Coach approach
And attitude of wearing Prada
It's about the passion
We have for fashion
Or the label mania obsession,
It's up to you, what's your impression?

We have become a material nation....

I'm Sorry

I'M SORRY

That you have to get the end result of a broken heart

I'M SORRY

That you have to see the side of a heart that's hard to mend.

I'M SORRY

That you have to endure the mind that will never trust
wholeheartedly, AGAIN.

I'M SORRY

Our hearts are uneven

I'M SORRY

It's me and to no one I can believe in

I'M SORRY

That you have to experience the weak side of my soul,

But in time unconditional love will take control.

And open a heart that has learned to trust and love again....

Money, Power, Respect

A man of many wonders
Trusting of me like a best friend with few limits,
Still afraid to tell all,
As anyone can imagine, for heart's safe keeping.
He holds a mild mannerism until his feet plant
Into his known workplace,
Bringing out some of the worst in him.
You could say he's pretty smart,
But most times has a selective memory.
A man who has huge dreams
Enjoying the finer things in life,
But doesn't live above his means.
He's a definite go-getter,
But for certain not a trend setter.
Needing more but settling for less
Accepting pearls when he deserves diamonds
Needing and wanting to connect the dots,
Missing some important pieces to his puzzle.
He knows where to find the key but has overlooked
The most important ingredient, still
Hoping he'll continue to conquer and be blessed,
With more money, power, respect....

My Outlet

My outlet
My tranquil time
It's what I use to relax my mind.
My love for expressing
My inner thoughts on paper,
Keeps me grounded.
Amazing myself of what lives deeply
Imbedded within me.
My soul sometimes, seemingly at a standstill
In time.
Not understanding why,
But hoping in time
It will reveal itself
And strangely enough it usually does
And it's not always easy.

Wanting so to express some thoughts aloud
But not given the opportunity,
Placing those thoughts in a bubble, in a cloud.
To play over and over in my head
Pondering over the thought of my
Words flowing aloud, would they be heard?
Or would they float through a crowd of air.
I've been told I find a deeper meaning
In words from another one's mouth,
Not that I purposely dissect their meaning
But I try my best to interpret with understanding.

My Pen Speaks for Me

These words lie deep within me, floating to the surface
For my pen to speak expressively,
These are the words my heart longs to speak
These are the words my heart wishes for.
The clock ticks as I'm running out of time
To complete these soulful expressions,
Before fading back into my safety deposit box.
I can't imagine these words forthcoming from my lips,
So I must compose these words on paper.
No exaggerations of the emotions,
Just reality buried deep, needing, wanting an outlet.
I've felt much pain; no more does my heart want to feel.
Exasperated I am, of these tireless, worldly games we play.
Pulling from every angle, seeking the next victim,
To cause insurmountable harm.
Though I struggle with my inner self,
and confidence of my ability,
That gives no one the right to say I won't, to say I can't.
Though they doubt to see me through I will continue to plant
The seed of success.
Though there are haters I'm determined to make
Them motivators. My mouth speaks it,
God will make it happen.
My dreams are larger than their imaginations.
Nobody knows the pain I've seen,
but many know how I've survived.
In the beginning with my head down,
but gained strength and overcame
The embarrassment and torment I felt would never fade.
The moment of truth is taking that last cry
and saving it for a happy time.
A time when the joy returns and I've fought
a hard battle and won.

On the Open Road

Traveling the open road
Windows down
Receiving the fresh air
Hours before the dawn
The perfect traveling hour
Few cars in sight
Traffic wide and free
Clear skies for miles
And miles ahead
No destination
Just open to go anywhere
The mind takes you
No hurry just sight-seeing
And exploring the possibilities
The imagination in a land
Of trees and earth without
Pollution and toxins to inhale

Like clouds in the night sky
So tranquil
No severe weather just a
Wave of rain that lasted
Only for a moment
Watching the waterfall from
The mountains so high
Now gazing upon the rainbow
Across the sky
Appreciating the value of life
As I continue my journey
And ride into the sun setting.

Racial Indifference

We see and then…we don't
We hear and then…we don't
We do and then…we don't
Our culture often has no justice
When we judge one another
From the beginning of time
Instead of leaving this behavior behind.
Going the distance
But still not a world of equal justice.
We inhale the same air.…
The same sunlight covers our bodies.…
And brings a different tone to our skin
The same shadow hovers over us
And brings back our unique color tone
Yes our cultures are different and…
There are those among us who won't acknowledge
There is racial indifference among us
Some of us want to love and bond equally
But our society makes it difficult to do
We cannot continue to pretend it's just me and you
Fighting the struggle is hard enough to do
Alone, wake up, we don't have to.
To be broken is to heal
To feel your heart mending to reveal
Your true heart's desire
We are strangers to one another's culture
We always need more grace in our face
To keep us grounded in faith.
We say we love the Lord and all that he stands for
But we repay him by differentiating and condemning,
Not loving unconditionally.
He created us all equally in the likeness of him
Though we are judgmental creatures,
Untouched by his sacrificing love
We pray to live in the likeness of him

But the opposite is what we portray.
The sound of gentle rain filling our hearts
Then the mystery of sudden despair
People; open your eyes in exchange for the divine.

Searching for My Butterflies

So difficult for me to be me
So busy being…, just being???
Some days I see and feel her trying to be free
Others, I search for that woman
Who used to smile all the time,
Who used to enjoy the simple
Pleasures of life.
Not feeling so controlled by
Climate and lighting
The constant reminder of restraint
Feelings of discomfort by the walls
That surrounds me.
Still searching for that woman
Who used to be happy-go-lucky
Even in times of stress and troubles of life,
Troubles of the world.
The happy days that sometimes
Didn't go as planned, but I made it through
Because I could smile and feel free,
Free even if I made mistakes.
Not feeling judged if I
Made the wrong move, made the wrong choice,
Made the wrong turn, made the wrong stop,
Chose the wrong words, chose the wrong tone.
If I can't be free to do these things then
What life am I living, who's life am I living,
Who's shadow am I portraying,
Who's image am I forming, who and what
Am I forced to be or who and what am I deciding
To become and for what purpose?
To maintain peace, but no peace of mind,
To maintain harmony, but there's little laughter
In my heart
To maintain the feeling of love, but less loved

I sometimes feel
To maintain communication, but communication
Only comes about when necessary
To maintain faith, because faith is all that I have left.
One day there will be no feelings of shame and
Continued search of acceptance because someday
I will make God proud that I am his child!
And my caterpillars will become butterflies!!!

The Forbidden

The urge was strong
The attraction was even stronger
But the committed heart beats fast within them
And they wanted to do the right thing
Realizing they had too much to loose
They both turned to close the door
And go the other way
The urge they have fought
And must feel no more.

An urge neither had felt in quite some time
It's almost as if a need from one
To the other lie beneath their skin
Their emotions flowing from the outside
Like the blood flowing through their veins
Second guessing their decision
The urge was strong but their faith was stronger.

To Freedom, to Justice, to Peace

The unspoken truth of oppression
turning ones blind eye
because it hasn't directly hit us
or for whatever reason we feel we must.
Do we think we have given so much of ourselves
that we don't need to help fight for justice.
The world has come from a dark place
but the shadows are still hovering over us
like the dark clouds before a storm.

We must stay dedicated to conquer equality
We need unity for our community
for our nation.
Challenge adversity
and accept what it has to offer in the end.
From the pain we will gain strength,
from the lessons learned we will gain knowledge
and with that knowledge
we will leave a legacy
not of defeat but of power.

From generation to generation
love and knowledge is all we have had,
we must give it in every way we know how
in every way possible.
Knowing life must be equal
let's break the sequel of separation.
Though the color of our skin may be different but
The blood that runs through every vein is red.
And without that one common denominator
we would not be.

The true definition of life is
love, freedom, peace, and
true justice, not to segregate
but connect the dots and get rid of the hate.

We can't control the trials and tribulations of life
but we can choose how we handle them.
As I've said and will keep saying
No matter what you've seen or heard
God has the final word.
He is the Victory!

Violence Lives Off of Silence

I dare you to breathe and tell a soul
About the first time I punched you
And left a hole
In your heart, only to break you
Down and give you no confidence and
Low self esteem.
Friends and family never realizing
Things are not always as they seem.
I dare you to have the heart to take control of your life
To put me in my place, the pain of my voice cuts like a knife.
To ensure I have you in my choke hold of violence,
To beat you unconscious to make my mold.
The pounding of my fist into your chest
And immediately after with the same hand
I give you my caress.
I plead my case of my sorrow
I never meant to hurt you; I'll make it up to you tomorrow.
I confess my love, sealed with a kiss
And dare you to pull back and resist
Knowing again you'll definitely meet my fist.
I dare you to take a stand and be strong
I dare you to speak out and prove me wrong.
You're in my institution, to be freed only by me,
Till death due us part is where you will be.
Until you break the silence
That has allowed the violence to live on.
Until you stop the violence that lives off of your silence.

Inspired by Sebrena B.T.

i know you're wondering
Who I'll Be Today???

Today you were what I know you can be
Tomorrow you'll fall short for whatever reason
I rejoiced and smiled wide yesterday
I cried today, longing for who you were the day before
Today I just pray for you to see me
Who knows what the focus of tomorrow will be
One day you're in a bliss, and the next day or so
you just dismiss
Me and vaguely push me away, sometimes
I don't even think you
Realize it, because you seem to believe everything is okay
because I'm smiling
But inside I'm a little confused, some days
it just comes natural
And others it's a struggle that doesn't have to be
If only you would open up to me
See and believe that I have you where no other can go
Do what a man does when he loves his woman
I'm your everything today
But tomorrow I will barely exist
You always amaze me when you toss the boomerang
And intertwine us in a twist, and somehow we end up
just hanging in the midst
Of a cliffhanger, dangling, wondering what next
I always keep an open mind
But I don't like the idea of hanging from a thin line....

Work Related—With No Intellect

Inside their minds
I have no desire to visit
Their thinking process
Feeds with no understanding
A thought process of senseless energy
Wasted, floating through
The air in which they breathe
Take a deep breath I say
Before the brain matter
Explodes from confusion
Having the illusion
That they can possibly figure out
What these files are all about.
Calculations running through the mind
Realizing math wasn't in their design.

Inside their minds
I have no desire to visit
The concept of value and price
Was never there or maybe just
A forgotten treasure
It's time to hire quality merchandise
To process scores and laws to be measured.
Future interviews should be questions of relevance
Attempting to be sure they can go the distance
To complete the job that involves detail
And complicated problem solving.
Not continuing to hire work-related
Applicants with no intellect.

Into My Father's Eyes

Looking into my father's eyes
Is like looking into my own
Watching him look intently
To see him as I walk closer
His pace and sway goes faster
As he recognizes a part of his
    seed approaching
No matter what the
    circumstances
I can see that he feels my love
He can see it in my eyes
Some of the greatest joys of
    past and present
Seeping through our smiles

I feel a distinctive look from him that he gives no other
My heart sometimes racing like its NASCAR's final lap
Looking back on life thinking and wishing we had walked
    together
Leaving our footprints in the sand
Maximizing a relationship that could have been so much more
Making us an ensemble that others wanted to be like
Dreams of sitting at our favorite café eating Russell Stover
    Candies
And Richard Munson Cinnabons without a calorie or care in
    the world
Locked on one another and bonding like glue stuck in that spot
With looks of a farmstead antique, rich in value and precious
    as jewels.

Live to Learn

The wrong way to be right
But no right way to be wrong
Classic lessons of the Bible
Hard lessons of the world
Before my time and after my rhyme
Using my body as a temple
To hold my poetic dictionary
Of soulful expressions
Personal training as I learn
From my own flow of terms
Regions of embedded knowledge
Finally beginning to make sense
In my daily existence
Changing the means of which I see
And understand
Signs of growth from awareness

Premium sounds echoing in my ear
The vibrations igniting something
In my brain, original words but new
Waves of expressions
No need to protect these words
Wanting all ears to hear
Wanting all eyes to see
My soul plastered on paper
Flowing from deep inside of me.

Simply Living

City living in my heart
Country girl in my soul
Touching the heart
Stirring the soul
Finding my mentors
And forming my mold
Branding my name
Embracing my life's role
Continuing my journey
Anticipating my star of gold
Learning to give more
And the return will triple fold
Teaching to go for it all
Not placing life on hold.

Who Moved My Chez?

Technically no one moved my chez
Because I never had any chez to be moved
Realistically speaking bills moved my chez
Because they are a never-ending cycle.
Gas prices and groceries moved my chez
And what little chez I had left to follow,
To enjoy simple pleasures of life.
Dreams of a lottery win
Embedded in my mind again and again
Not to be rich, but comfortable
Slicing the bread and rolling the dice
Losing the bet and paying the price,
Never skipping what's due
To buy something new
Not knowing where my next piece of chez
Would come from,
Living from check to check
And still a list of things to neglect.
Trying so hard to stay afloat
Feelings of sinking in quicksand
But not totally drowning
But wallowing, not in self-pity
But putting the pride aside
And ducking and dodging to hide
The urge to cry and fall apart
Because I had to stay strong
For the other mouths I had to feed
And other bodies I had to lead.
Depending on me to get them through
Choosing between food or paying what's past due,
Splitting the decision and doing both
And awaiting the next chunk of chez
From Uncle Sam's tax season
To try and get a little ahead of the game
So I could rest my mind and continue the chain,

With high hopes of prosperity
And achieving my goals.
God leads me and perseverance feeds me
As I continue to dwell, life is now treating me well!

The Element of Design

I'm in my zone
Texting and talking on the phone
Thriving as I drive my dreams
Through my words that theme
My life, my run, as I race
My highs, my lows
While I begin to know
Which direction to go
Which way to turn
As I burn the midnight hour
Turning the pages as my fingers
Continue to write and fill the spaces
Until there is no more.
Wanting to keep going
But there is nothing that I can do
To keep my eyelids apart
So I put my pen to rest for awhile,
To refresh my brain for a new start.
Ancient words but new ideas of my design
Where many writers have gone but created
Their one of a kind creation
And demonstration of expressions,
Of how we interpret the exact same lesson.
Always searching for a new story to tell
Hoping to enlighten the mind that
Didn't grasp it the first or second time
Through its original design.

So Distant, Yet So Close

So hard to live in this world of…doubt, hopelessness,
    separation, and self pity,

The ambition to lead a life of quality
Not really enough of us seeking the knowledge
He has given us, knowing knowledge is power
What are we all waiting on?
We frequently put things of importance on hold
Many times we reconnect with the idea
And so many times it's a little late.

Heaven often seems so far away
But can be as close as tomorrow
At the end of our course
We want to see him
Though we loose sight of him
We doubt him, we question him
But yet we still believe in him.

So hard to live in this world so … just trust, pray, come
    together, and believe….

Lower Level, Higher Ground

So many phases of life
Which direction would they have gone?
With no intrusion
Which direction would they have gone?
If all people were genuinely happy
And no man would tread on another.

People departing out of hurt and anger
People departing over what someone else has said
Over partial truths and lies that another mouth has spread
First loves of the young mind
Never realizing the true signs
Of separation that comes with gossip and jealousy of mankind.

Had our hearts been more mature
Not to stumble to lower levels
But to climb to higher grounds
To block the haters that impede
Causing one to leave behind first true love
That could have been
What no one ever knows but leaving one to ponder
Leaving one to wonder what we could have done
What we should have done
The mature mind would have talked it out
To find out what all the nonsense was about.

Two people who have moved beyond the hurt and pain
Not to remain friends but to regain poise
From all the noise that was planted in their ears
And reconnect on a different level from all the wasted and lost
    years
Two people who lived their lives on separate foundations
Finally coming back together with understanding
With perceptive minds never to allow another man's words
To come between them again.

Is She Listening?

Is she listening?
Does she hear me when I speak?
Is she watching over me?
Does she see the tears that fill my eyes,
When she is a constant in my mind?

Does she know the reason why parts of me exist?
Does she feel my struggle to stay afloat
When I need to hear her gentle voice?
Does she know that the love I have
For her is deeper than one can imagine?
Does she hear my cry when troubles come my way?
Does she still hear me, can she see my face
Through the clouds as she walks across the sky?
Does she still say, "Pick your head up and remain strong."
I think I hear her voice whispering in my ear
Baby girl, I'm listening, I hear.

My Time to Go...

It was my time to go
You may not think the time was right
But God cleared my mind and kept me from the fight,
He gave me courage to end painful days and restless nights.

He lifted my spirit and set me free
Trust me, it was my time to go, this you must see.
The sadness you feel, replace it with the times we've shared
Turn your tears to sunshine
And in that rainbow you shall see my face
Full of joy and laughter
To be re-assured I've lived my life in good character.

The emotional bond we shared never ends
And I'll continue to hold your place in my heart
Because the body dies but the soul never parts.
And for every ending there is a new beginning....

Release Me

As I leave this world, release me and let go
There are great plans for me in a future you're sure to know,
Be content that I have earned my crown
As I enter into heaven and hear the horns' sound
Welcoming me with praise.

Know that the love and joy that we've shared
Was the best time I had here on earth
And has helped prepare me for a better place called heaven

Continue to live out your destined path
So you'll leave cherishing memories that last,
I won't be as far as you may think
So if you need to talk I'll be listening.

Always remember that one day we will
Cross the same path again
And I'll be waiting with my arms open
And my heart warm
I'll see you when Heaven's gates open for you.

Wishing on a Star

Wishing on a star, the focus is not yet clear
But will become more visible, as the dawn appears
Or maybe at the next sunset to beautiful skies
And no clouds to shadow its glow
The memories I want etched in my mind
To never forget such a tranquil moment in time.

With You....

Wishing you could love me for life
Solid as you stand when you take my hands
Into the palm of your own
Our transparent gift to the other
Works well in our peculiar world
Though the love I have for you
Still aches though I know you're with me
Wanting that constant to never fade.
You're with me as one as my heart skips a beat
When my mind ponders are we concrete.
I sometimes feel insecure because of your lack of
Gentle touches but constant expressions of love.
Trying to be a man of your word as you make an effort to
    please
Me but really still trying to figure it out
We've held a silent love that lie dormant for a few years
Though dormant, still breathing and alive
Searching for the pursuit of true happiness
While allowing it to fade into some of its darkest nights
Settling for less but deserving of so much more

Never believing our paths
Would cross again at the exact same bridge
At the exact same time
Paying for our worldly possessions
But it remains to be seen whether we will
Ever gain our priceless treasure to love and happiness

With You....

I Surrender

Jesus came
When I was broken
Changed my way of thinking
Took away the pain
To show me sunlight after the rain
Freed my mind of fear and doubt
All I had to do was call
He came and gave his all
And that's why I surrender all.
Stayed faithful
As He gave me twice as much
He was in my reach just not to the touch
In my spiritual attitude
Stayed strong, grew wiser
He was my advisor, never denying me
Of his enormous reward
So once and for all
I've removed my guard.

He's never slow on his promises
My breakthrough was coming
Trusting and believing he would open that door
Never gave up, he had always kept his promises before
Just didn't come when I wanted
But came just in a matter of time
I knew his name
Stopped calling it in vain
I knew his name
I've called and he has regained
As I've changed
He has remained the same
Kept seeking
And he kept meeting
My needs to be free
Kept believing even when it got hard
And it will remain between me and God.

The Sound of Laughter

The sound of laughter
Children dying of disaster
Praying daily
Laying it all in the hands of our master.
The touch of a small hand
In the palm of your own,
For seeing their future
Admiring how they have grown.
Feeling great satisfaction
From their wide smiles
And innocent eyes,
Their energy and spunk, so alive.
And then the unexpected attack
Of life accompanied by crisis,
Pain in their faces
You had never imagined possible.
The pain begins

But seems never ending,
Hearts breaking, never mending.
Minimizing the simple joys of life
Igniting life's strife.
Their serenity, their purity
Shines a bright light in a dark world,
In our world of sorrow
They are visions of tomorrow.

Weathering the Storm

From years past
Knowing family history
Of a striking disaster
That takes us by surprise
That took her to her resting place
I understood it was God's grace
Where he wanted her to be
Her children saddened and in pain
From the treacherous wind that had been
Blown into their lives
Always on my mind
Whether it would strike twice
Every emotion imaginable
Every emotion is real
Your thoughts run rampant
And takes over your daily way of functioning
You travel to a place where no one else
Is there and dares to imagine
A cold and lonely feeling
A state of mind that feels as if
It began to rain and hail, never ending
And even when the first boat was sent to your rescue
You climbed in and felt safe for as long as it lasted
You fall again and somehow you float ashore
And after what seems like a century has passed
The Savior that was always there
Is waiting for you to allow him in.
Allow him to defend your flesh
Allowing you to cease the restless days
And sleepless nights
Before He reaches you
Anger sets in and you wonder why
What have you done in life
To weather this storm
To have been cut deep

Riddled, hurting, stricken with grief
Questioning God, even though His faith has
Always been a part of us, still confused
Trying to grasp your breath and get to a place
In knowing God would guide you to that peace.

RIP Aunt Sherri Dozier

Parent vs. Child

Mind over matter
As we pick our battles
The ship is not wrecked
Until we sink so low
The habits of our bickering mouths
Because we don't try hard enough
Or we don't know how.

Bowing down and knowing your place
Will always keep you in God's grace
Though times with parent vs. child
Are always challenging
It's all about love, peace, and
Giving more of yourself
While balancing.

As you seek peace from an endless
War worth fighting
Because the love is there
Though sometimes we hide it
Searching our soul to rid the curt tongue
Or our children who are more prone
To snap back at you if you allow them to.

Setting the rules is the key
Though they may disagree
God appoints parents as guidance to their destiny
And there is no reward for disobedience
But great pleasure in knowing
You've done your part
In satisfying them both
As you continue to grow
Into adulthood and remain
Forever in their hearts.

Kwansaba Poetry

The kwansaba, a forty-nine-word poetic form invented during the Writers Club's 1995 workshop season (in East St. Louis), consists of seven lines of seven words each, with no word containing more than seven letters. (Think 7-7-7!) Exceptions to the seven-letter rule are proper nouns and some foreign terms. Previous issues of "Drumvoices Review" have featured kwansabas for Miles Davis (2003), Katherine Dunham (2004), Amiri Baraka and Sonia Sanchez (2005), Jayne Cortez (2006), Maya Angelou and Quincy Troupe (2007) and Richard Wright (2008).

The Break Away

He broke away from life's cycles. A
path that demands nothing, aiming to achieve
vital dreams, he prepared for this place
of the unknown. To believe in the
fortune it may bring. Not of pesos
but riches of honor to leave behind.
He flew with wings to his throne.

No Hidden Sorrow

No hidden sorrow, just selling his power
with intense words, to compel the world
for a small ransom. Bowing down to
an awesome journey, to build and leave
a spell bond legacy. Leaving his mind
but only for a moment, coming back
still standing, a kingdom he had won.

A Race Won

He looked to the sky, the never
ending clouds signal no limits to prosper.
His energy forced him ahead. Running his
marathon like a whirl wind tornado chasing.
Miles of road ahead, count down, time
ticking, waiting for no one. The race
was on and he won with grace.

Release for Life

He an artist, lyrics blessed. Given in
voice with written passion, the search for
life's visuals, going forward in maximum speed.
To explore his texture and riches, chances
for a greater success. And he wanted
nothing less than to retreat into clouds
through images of poetry, a galaxy created.

Success

Turned the pages of life, he did.
Capture, strive, pulsate to become a legacy.
Stories of few words, but the message
so large. The soul of hunger as
he thirsts for his cup to over
flow. Racing to gulp as much as
he could stomach, to drown in success.

Eternal Life

Scent of candles flicker as she goes
through the process, trying not to deprive
herself of comfort, hard in spirit, tough
in love. Shaving her rough edges with
primer to become a soulful mixture of
a fruit filled flower to blossom, with
no help from water, she submits to God.

Voice of a Soldier

Voice of a soldier saying no more
war, path of an honest heart wanting
to connect again with loved ones. Plead
for mercy to a higher power. He
has grown not weak but drained from
worldly torment, he is the hero worthy
of release from bondage, like the enemy.

Defeat with Power

Quiet spirit of song birds, sounds of
melody to calm the beast within, prior
roars of thunder like quakes spillin' over.
No valleys left behind, just mud and
clay with no resting place. The ruins
of Katrina were crushed souls but over
coming defeat with more power than ever.

The Drug War

Here today but taken over, blind sided
by the drug of choice to mask
the pain. Feeling no pain, drowned in
self pity with no pure air to
breathe, mull over coming to your senses
only to be pulled again but rising
upon that last hope for life.

Material Loss, Love Gained

Pushing, still falling short, having to pack
and uproot from your place called home
to go where he needed you to.
Eyes still closed without a clue of
why you, but the reason has been
exposed and your mind still not clear
but seeming to grasp what must be.

My Truth

When I speak, hear my voice, sense
the power and spread the words I
extend to you, believe in me for
all I do is try to give
truth, though truth you may not want
but it must be in order to
release the baggage you hold within you.

READERS' COMMENTS

As always, AWESOME! It amazes me how you are able to express yourself in this manner. All I can say is Little Maya A.
—Sidney C. Sessoms, Jr-Livingstone College

Patrice,
Your website is very nice, and inspirational.
Kind Regards,
—Renee, Consumer Relations, StrideRite

Congratulations! What an honor! I pray the DrumVoices exposure will be a blessing beyond your wildest dreams.
Hugs,
—Paul Butler, Jr.-Pastor (Connector Christian Fellowship)

Thanks Mrs. Watley-Williams . . . and strength to your writin' hand.
Easy,
—Professor Eugene B. Redmond

Mrs. P.,
This poem is absolutely one of the best I have ever read. You are indeed a talented young lady. God has really smiled on you. Please hang in there and don't ever give up on your writing passion. You are destined to be great.
Be Blessed, Your Friend
—B Darrington

I just did a search on you to see what you have done with your trailer. VERY GOOD SHOW, my friend. You have been busy. I wish all our clients did that. Excellent job! I saw it in a lot of places.
—Sandra Rea, Book Candy Studios

Ha . . . you got down with that one. I could hear the sax playing in the background . . . love it.

—Isaac McKenzie

Another nice work of art! So glad to be in your circle.

—Deborah Johnson

Hey Patrice! You're like wine, you just keep getting better and better with time! I love it!

—Lashannon A. Spencer

Absolutely flawless. I think its a superb work of literature; there you go, you did it again!

—Roger McLean

BEAUTIFUL!

—Akieria T. Hall

Patrice, what a good reminder and a beautiful way to start the morning! Thank you for tagging me on this.

—Rene Miller

Patrice, this is almost biblical…it'll preach all by itself! I really enjoy your poetry, you should author another book!

—Marque Rosser

Family oriented, still manages to make your mark in the artistry world of poetry. You are beautifully talented; genuinely devoted to those that have the honor to make their way into your heart. A rare gem, indeed.

—Brook Blander, Author/Designer

About the Author

Patrice Watley-Williams believes that everyone has a purpose and knows that we find in life exactly what we put into it. She understands that anything worth fighting for is never in vain, and learning to take a deeper look keeps us from neglecting a life of possibilities. Continuing to love and embrace her trials as well as her successes, Patrice indulges in her craft and passion for writing what she considers her "Phases of Life" with a purpose.

As an author, she is inspired by many famous and infamous authors; but one who has taught her a new phase of poetry, called Kwansaba, is Professor Eugene B. Redmond, Editor Drum Voices Revue. Patrice also has written song lyrics for Grafted by Grace Contemporary Christian Recording Artist and a local Atlanta Jazz Band, as well as purpose statements for non-profit organizations. Her prior published work is *Perseverance From the Heart/Poetic Mind Vibes* and her poetry appeared in the compilation entitled *Colors of Life*. She is currently working on her next books, *Faces in the Mirror* and *Lyrically Speaking*. Mrs. Watley-Williams lives with her husband and her children, in Marietta, Georgia. As she moves onward, her purpose filled journey is to leave a small marked legacy.

CPSIA information can be obtained at www.ICGtesting.com
Printed in the USA
LVOW070306160911

246536LV00001B/75/P